THE CLASSICS OF GOLF

Edition of

THE
BASIC GOLF
SWING

Text by Robert T. Jones, Jr.
Illustrations by Anthony Ravielli

Foreword by Herbert Warren Wind
Afterword by Charles R. Yates

ISBN 0-940889-29-3

Foreword

Shortly after Time, Inc. had launched its weekly sports magazine, Sports Illustrated, *in the summer of 1954, the decision was made to run a regular golf-instruction feature called "Tip from the Top" in which professional golfers and golf professionals from all parts of the United States provided the tips. Jerome Snyder, the magazine's art editor, selected Anthony Ravielli to illustrate this feature. Ravielli, who happened to be an enthusiastic golfer, was known for the skill of his anatomical drawings. He was the master of a difficult technique called scratchboard in which the artist makes his drawings in Higgins' India Ink on gesso-coated paper and then scrapes out the white lines with a miniature shovel. It was almost instantly apparent that Ravielli's work had created a new standard of excellence in the field of golf instruction. He went on to raise the level of his art with his inspired work on Ben Hogan's "The Modern Fundamentals of Golf", which first appeared in five installments in* Sports Illustrated *in the late winter and early spring of 1957.*

After "Tip from the Top" had wound down in 1960, Ravielli began a long and happy relationship with Golf Digest *magazine that has continued down to the present. However, the bulk of his time, as had always been the case, was devoted to writing and illustrating books. In the 1950s and 1960s he produced a superb succession of children's books for Viking Press, among them "Wonders of the Human Body", "An Adventure in Geometry", an astronomy book called "The World Is Round", a book on evolution called "From Fins to Hands", "The Rise of the Dinosaurs", and "Elephants, the Last of the Land Giants". In the 1960s he wrote and illustrated four children's books for Atheneum: "What Is Bowling?", "What Is Golf?", "What Is Tennis?", and "What Are Street Games?". In the 1960s, he illustrated two books written by Isaac Asimov, "The Human Body" and "The Human Brain". During the last two decades he has worked on a number of books on scientific and medical subjects that were published by Lippincott. His golf assignments have served as a welcome change of pace.*

In the middle 1960s, Charles Price, the golf writer, got in touch with Ravielli. Price was working with Robert T. Jones, Jr., the great champion, in putting together a collection of the instructional features that Jones had written for the Bell Syndicate between 1927 and 1935. The material that Price, the editor, selected for "Bobby Jones on Golf", as the book was called, came to approximately eighty thousand words. Ravielli supplied a page of superior illustrations for each of the fourteen chapters. Doubleday and Company published the book in 1965. Ravielli subsequently contracted with Doubleday to work, with Jones's assistance, on a book that would describe and depict Jones's classic golf swing. Ravielli first selected the sections of the text of "Bobby Jones on Golf" that he thought should be illustrated. Taking a relatively standard approach, he divided the book into ten chapters: The Grip; The Stance; The Start of the Backswing; The Top of the Backswing; The Start of the Downswing; The Downswing; Impact; The Follow Through; A Review; and, interestingly, to bring out its importance, a sort of curtain call entitled Striking the Ball.

When the project was well underway, Ravielli made several trips to Atlanta and met with Jones in the offices of his law firm, Jones, Bird, and Howell. Jones at this time was moving into his late sixties and was not in the best of health, but he was extremely cooperative. He arranged for Ravielli and himself to watch the original films of "How I Play Golf", the instruction series he had made for Warner Brothers in 1931. He got together a good deal of material that he thought might be of help to Ravielli. This included his instruction articles for The American Golfer magazine and the famous stroboscopic stop-action photographs of his swing that were made at the Massachusetts Institute of Technology. Jones went over Ravielli's "roughs"—his preparatory drawings—with the utmost care and suggested some minor changes. He made a number of alterations in his original text to clarify certain points he wanted to make. Jones also wrote a characteristically generous foreword for "Bobby Jones on the Basic Golf Swing", as the book was called. It concludes with this short paragraph: "Without disclaiming responsibility for the descriptive writing in this book, I want it understood that, above all else, this book belongs to Tony Ravielli. If it succeeds in its purpose, such success will be due to the eloquence of Tony's art."

Ravielli illustrated "Bobby Jones on the Basic Golf Swing" with line drawings and sepia overlays. He also did the layouts of the individual pages. The book, the ultimate depiction of Jones's method of hitting the golf ball, was published in 1969. As a boy growing up on the course of the East Lake Golf Club in Atlanta, Jones had copied the long Carnoustie swing of Stewart Maiden, the club's Scottish-born professional, with its full, free hip-turn. From a distance, the members were never certain who they were watching, Maiden or Jones, their swings were so similar. In the opinion of many authorities on the golf swing, Jones's swing on his tee shots was overly long. At the top of the backswing when he was playing his driver, the shaft of the club actually dipped below the point where it was parallel to the ground. This, to be sure, is a dangerous position, but Jones had the ability to keep the club well *under control. He started his downswing by unwinding his hips, and, with his excellent balance and timing, he released the tremendous power he had stored up as he unloaded on the ball. (Jones explains his hitting action in considerable detail in this book.) Jones's long swing worked for him, but he was careful not to suggest that it would suit the average golfer. When he made his series of instruction films in Hollywood, he made it a point to call it "How I Play Golf", not "How To Play Golf". He appreciated that, while certain fundamental movements are present in the swings of all the best golfers, each champion has an individual style that works for him. Jones was not a big man—stocky in build, he stood about five feet eight—but he executed his long swing with such control and precision that he was not only a very accurate player but the longest hitter of his day. It was thrilling to watch him, because his lyrical tempo and his gracefulness made his powerful swing appear to be effortless.*

Everyone knows the general pattern of Jones's career in golf. At nine he won the junior championship at the East Lake Golf Club. At fourteen he captured the Georgia State Amateur, and his dad rewarded him by letting him go up to Merion in 1916 and play in the United States Amateur. He won his first two matches, and in the next round he carried the defending champion, Bob Gardner, to the thirty-third green. It took Jones a long time, however, to master his high-strung temperament, and he didn't win a national championship until 1923, when he at last broke through in the United States Open. After that, there was no stopping him. During the next seven years, he led the way in an even dozen major championships. In 1930, after sweeping the British Amateur, the British Open, the United States Open, and the United States Amateur, in that order, he had the uncommon good sense to retire from competitive golf at twenty-eight.

What made Bobby Jones so rare, however, was that Jones the person was every bit as exceptional as Jones the golfer. He had an unusually fine mind that was not unlike Thomas Jefferson's in the width of its range. He first thought he would like to be a mechanical engineer. In 1919, he entered Georgia Tech at seventeen, and he received his B. S. degree after completing the four-year course in three years. By that time, he knew that a career in mechanical engineering was not what he wanted. (He made good use of that training when, after his retirement from tournament golf, he undertook to design Jones-model golf clubs for the A. G. Spalding Company.) In the autumn of 1922, Jones enrolled at Harvard. During the next two years, he took a variety of courses in history, modern languages, and English literature. After concluding this special course of studies, he received a second B. S. degree. He then returned to Atlanta. The son of a lawyer, Jones subsequently entered Emory University Law School, in Atlanta. Halfway through his second year, he passed the Georgia State bar exams and began to practice law.

I have an idea that the two years that Jones spent at Harvard may have been especially valuable for a young man of his marked sensibility. I would imagine that the lecturers he sat before, the books he read, and the company of the pleasantly intellectual but well-rounded students with whom he became friends opened broad new vistas for him. The odds are that he would never have developed his splendid talent for writing if he had not been exposed at just the right time to this stimulating new world. Having already graduated from college, Jones did not play golf for Harvard, but a number of the friends he made there were golfers who admired him for his charming manner and lively mind as much as they did for the position he held in the game. It was during this period, I would guess, that Jones learned to speak well and easily on his feet. He practically invented the traditional informal acceptance speech that American sports heroes deliver at presentation ceremonies. In some degree, his two happy years at Harvard may also have accounted for the quickness with which he came to feel so much at home in Great Britain. The Scots and the English were crazy about him. He had been elected a member of the Royal & Ancient Golf Club of St. Andrews before he won the British Open on the Old Course in 1927, and he delighted the members of the club, the townspeople of St. Andrews, and golfers around the world when, instead of taking the trophy back to Atlanta, he left it in the safekeeping of the R. & A.

For the people of St. Andrews, Jones was the dream golfer they had been waiting for. They did not discover each other in 1921 when Jones lost his self-control in the Open championship and picked up his ball on the eleventh hole on the third round. However, the extraordinary love affair between Jones and the people of St. Andrews was clearly observable on his later visits: in 1926, when the Walker Cup match was held there; in 1927, when he won the British Open on the Old Course with a sterling performance; in 1930, when he won the British Amateur there and gave himself a shot at the Grand Slam; and in 1936 when, en route to the Olympic Games in Berlin, he popped into town unannounced for a round of golf and was soon joined on the Old Course by four thousand friends and admirers. This relationship reached its apex in the autumn of 1958 when Jones returned to St. Andrews as the captain of the American team in the inaugural playing of the World Amateur Team Championship. On this visit, the Freedom of the City and the Royal Borough of St. Andrews was conferred on Jones, the first American to be so honored since Benjamin Franklin in 1759. The ceremony took place in Younger Hall one evening during the championship. A crowd of seventeen hundred, the large majority of them townspeople, crowded into the auditorium, filling it literally to the rafters. At the conclusion of a first-rate welcoming speech by the Provost of St. Andrews, Jones, deeply moved by the manifest affection of the gathering, decided not to use the notes he had made and spoke extemporaneously for about ten minutes. He said a number of unforgettable things, including these:

(About the Old Course) "You have to study it, and the more you study it, the more you learn; the more you learn, the more you study it."

"You people of St. Andrews have a sensitivity and an ability to extend cordiality in an ingenious way."

"I could take out of my life everything except my experiences at St. Andrews and I still would have had a rich and full life."

"I just want to say to you that this is the finest thing that has ever happened to me . . . I like to feel about it this way: that now I officially have the right to feel at home in St. Andrews as much as I, in fact, have always done."

As Jones prepared to leave the hall at the conclusion of his talk, the townspeople in Younger Hall rose to their feet and began to sing the old Scottish folk song, "Will Ye No' Come Back Again?". They did this with profound emotion, and their voices had the fierce, wild sound of an ancient pibroch played by pipers echoing up some distant glen.

I came to know Bob Jones fairly well, mainly because I was a good friend of Al Laney's. Laney covered golf and tennis and many other sports for the Paris Herald and the New York Herald Tribune for over four decades, beginning in the 1920s. As a young man, he was *gassed in the Allies' final offensive in the First World War, and many months passed before he was considered well enough to return to the States. That took place in 1919. En route to his hometown of Pensacola, Laney, still in uniform, stopped off in Atlanta to watch Jones play in the Southern Open. His imagination had been fired by the accounts he had read of the young man's unusual talent and manner. He got to speak with Jones and found him all that he hoped he would be. After Laney's discharge from the army, he was hired by the Atlanta bureau of the Associated Press. His work there led him to set up an appointment to interview Jones, who at that time was attending Georgia Tech and living at his college fraternity house. The evening Laney went over to see Jones, he was seated on a large sofa at one end of the front porch and engaged in a conversation with friends. Laney made his way over to the group and, introducing himself to Jones, said that they had met at the Southern Open but that Jones probably didn't remember it. Jones broke into a warm smile. "Mister Laney," he said, "you're not as forgettable as you may think you are."*

During the middle and late 1920s, Laney was the one American sportswriter who regulary was on hand to cover the deeds of Jones and Bill Tilden on both sides of the Atlantic. He got to know Tilden as well as any tennis writer ever did, and he and Jones were devoted to each other. In the early 1950s, after Jones had undergone two major operations, he was informed that he had a crippling spinal disease, syringomyelia. Jones somehow managed to live with it until December, 1971, when he died at sixty-nine. One April morning in the early 1950s just previous to the start of play in the Masters, Jones was sitting in his golf cart near the clubhouse at Augusta National when Laney came over to say hello. Jones asked him to sit in the cart with him. He then drove to a part of the course where they would be by themselves. "Al, there is something I should tell you," Jones said. "I have come down with a serious illness. There is no chance of my getting better. It can only get worse. I want you to know this. Now, from this point on, we're not going to talk about it again." The two friends looked at each other for a long time. Down through the years, Jones and Laney had many lengthy chats together, but Jones's illness was never mentioned.

Jones made golf a major preoccupation throughout the South, and there is no question that his immense popularity was responsible for the large number of able young Southern amateurs who came to the front. Three in particular are closely identified with Jones. The first was Watts Gunn. He was about three years younger than Jones and grew up, like Jones, at the East Lake Golf Club. In 1925, when the U.S. Amateur was scheduled to be held at Oakmont, near Pittsburgh, Jones persuaded Watts' parents to let him take a crack at the championship. That year, a new format was used in the Amateur. Only the low sixteen scorers qualified for the rounds at match play, and all the matches were over thirty-six holes. Twenty-year-old Watts Gunn had a terrific week. He qualified handily for the match-play rounds. Playing stupendous golf, he won his first match 12 and 10, his second 10 and 9, and his third 5 and 3. This took him to the final where he met Jones. For a time, Jones had his hands full. However, a burst of birdies at the end of the morning round got him rolling, and he then went on to close out the match, 8 and 7. Gunn was a good, solid golfer. While he was at Georgia Tech, he won the National Intercollegiate championship in 1927, and he also won the Georgia State Amateur and the Southern Amateur. He was a member of our Walker Cup team in 1926 and 1928, and captured his two singles and his two foursomes by emphatic margins.

The second Southern amateur linked with Jones is Billy Joe Patton. A native of Morgantown, North Carolina, and a graduate of Wake Forest University, Patton was just another good amateur until he caught fire in the 1954 Masters. The two best players of that day, Ben Hogan and Sam Snead, had to summon their very best stuff to edge him out by a stroke in the final round. (In their playoff, Snead defeated Hogan, 70 to 71.) Patton's daring golf and his engaging manner kept him in the public eye. He tied for twelfth in the 1956 Masters, finished eighth in 1958, and tied for eighth the following year. He was the low amateur in the U. S. Open in 1954 at Baltusrol and in 1956 at Inverness. He was a prominent member of our Walker Cup team in 1955, 1957, 1959, 1963, and 1965, and he captained the team in 1969. He was a member of the American team that Jones captained in the first World Amateur Team championship at St. Andrews in 1958, and he was in the audience at Younger Hall the historic night that the freedom of the city was conferred on Jones. (At the conclusion of this ceremony, he wasn't able to speak for several minutes.) Patton was an impressive driver, he could devise wonderful clutch shots with the pitching wedge, he could putt, and he could compete. He also went about playing golf as if it were the greatest pleasure in the world, and he was liked and admired as deeply in Britain as he was in this country.

Last but not least, there was Charlie Yates, a bright and discerning Atlantan, who won our National Intercollegiate championship in 1934 when he was attending Georgia Tech. Yates was a member of the American team that shut out the British and Irish in the Walker Cup match at Pine Valley in 1936. His big year was 1938. He carried off the British Amateur at Troon, edging by Hector Thomson, the accomplished Scottish player, on the first extra hole in the semifinals, and taking the final, 3 and 2, from Cecil Ewing, of

Ireland. Right on the heels of this, in the Walker Cup match at St. Andrews, Yates, partnered with Ray Billows, won his foursomes, and the following day he defeated James Bruen, the very talented young Irishman, in the top singles. Britain and Ireland won the team match, seven points to four, to gain its first victory in the series. At the presentation ceremony, the Scottish gallery called for Yates, who had gone undefeated in Scotland, and he responded with typical brio by leading the crowd in a rousing chorus of "A Wee Doch an' Dorris".

Charlie Yates has been kind enough to provide the Afterword for "The Basic Golf Swing". Yates was about a dozen years younger than Jones, but they got to know each other early and they knew each other well. Like Jones, Yates has played a significant role in international golf. He captained the American Walker Cup team in the match at Kittansett in 1953, and he was the honorary captain of our team in the match at Pine Valley in 1985. When the fiftieth anniversary of the Walker Cup series was celebrated on the eve of the match at St. Andrews in 1971, Yates was asked to serve as master of ceremonies at the gala dinner attended by a huge turnout of former Walker Cup players. His wit and his sense of the significance of the occasion made the evening glow. He is one of the persons who gives the week of the Masters its unique flavor. He and his brother Dan have for decades handled the player interviews in the Press Building at Augusta National. On Saturday morning, he conducts the annual meeting of the Jones Memorial Scholarship Committee at which the star turns are the informal talks by the Jones scholars from St. Andrews University who are attending Emory University. On Saturday evening, he and his wife Dorothy are the hosts at the dinner for the British golf writers. Late on Sunday, when the pace of the long week is beginning to tell on just about everyone, Yates, somehow or other, manages to remain as perky as ever. Wearing that rueful smile of his and winking from time to time at old friends, he is the picture of ease as he takes the winner of the tournament in hand at the beginning of his press interview, checks the microphone, and says, "Fellers, as you can see, we've got the new Masters champion here for you. What do you want him to do first, go over the highlights of his round or go over his round hole by hole?"

BOBBY JONES ON THE BASIC GOLF SWING

Over a period of eight years, until he retired at the
youthful age of twenty-eight in 1930, BOBBY JONES
dominated the golf scene. In that short span of time he
won the United States Amateur five times, the United
States Open four times, the British Open three times and
the British Amateur once. His unforgettable Grand Slam
of 1930, when he won all four major titles in one golfing
season, remains the outstanding achievement in the
history of the game.

BOBBY JONES
on
THE
BASIC GOLF
SWING

by
ROBERT TYRE (BOBBY) JONES

illustrated by
ANTHONY RAVIELLI

1969
DOUBLEDAY & COMPANY, INC.
GARDEN CITY, NEW YORK

Books by Bobby Jones

DOWN THE FAIRWAY *(with O. B. Keeler)*
GOLF IS MY GAME
BOBBY JONES ON GOLF
BOBBY JONES ON THE BASIC GOLF SWING

Library of Congress Catalog Card Number: 89-12853
Text Copyright © 1969 by Robert Tyre Jones, Jr.
Illustrations Copyright © 1969 by Anthony Ravielli
All Right Reserved
Printed in the United States of America
First Edition

FOREWORD

This is a picture book; a book of drawings by the perceptive Tony Ravielli illustrating excerpts from my own writings on golf. To me, the drawings make the book.

I think the drawings are more revealing than photographs, because in them is expressed the artist's interpretation of the movement, as well as my own. Although each drawing illustrates a position, it also is capable of indicating whence the position was derived and in what direction will be the departure.

The aim of the book is to provide a series of images which will communicate to the golfer a meaningful picture of the correct action at various stages of the golf stroke.

I have often said that the essence of good form is simplicity; in turn, simplicity is brought about by the elimination of faults or unnecessary movements. The pictures in this book, together with the text, are intended to direct the player straight to his goal. Admittedly, he may accomplish good results by compensating for failures in technique. But a more reliable performance must result if the failures are eliminated, so that the compensations become unnecessary.

It is not possible, and no attempt is made, to prescribe the limits or the force of any action. The only prescription offered is of the proper order of movement. The artist and I together have tried to show how the golfer may most effectively and reliably move into his backswing, change smoothly from the backward movement into the striking effort, and then deliver the blow precisely and explosively at the back of the ball. If this is done, all else will fit into an agreeable picture.

Without disclaiming responsibility for the descriptive writing in this book, I want it understood that, above all else, this book belongs to Tony Ravielli. If it succeeds in its purpose, such success will be due to the eloquence of Tony's art.

ROBERT T. JONES, JR.

CONTENTS

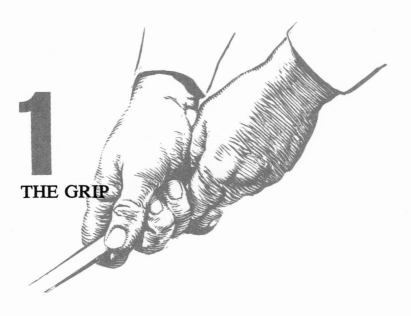

1

THE GRIP

A correct grip is a fundamental necessity in the golf swing. It might even be said to be the first necessity, for a person must take hold of the club before he can swing it, and he must hold it correctly before it becomes physically possible for him to swing it correctly.

In the correct grip, the two hands should be able to function as nearly as possible as one, and their placement should encourage easy handling of the club throughout the swing. The golfer must also maintain a fixed relation throughout the swing between his hands and the face of the club. Obviously, the shaft must not turn in his hands while he is making the stroke. So his grip must be positive and firm but not strained.

If a player is not in the habit of employing a grip that fills this bill, he should immediately alter it until it does; but after altering his grip until it is correct and comfortable, let him resolve never to change it. If something goes wrong, let him look elsewhere for the trouble, for the hands form the connection with the club; through the hands the player is able to sense the location and alignment of the club; they are the key to his control; the slightest change leaves him groping.

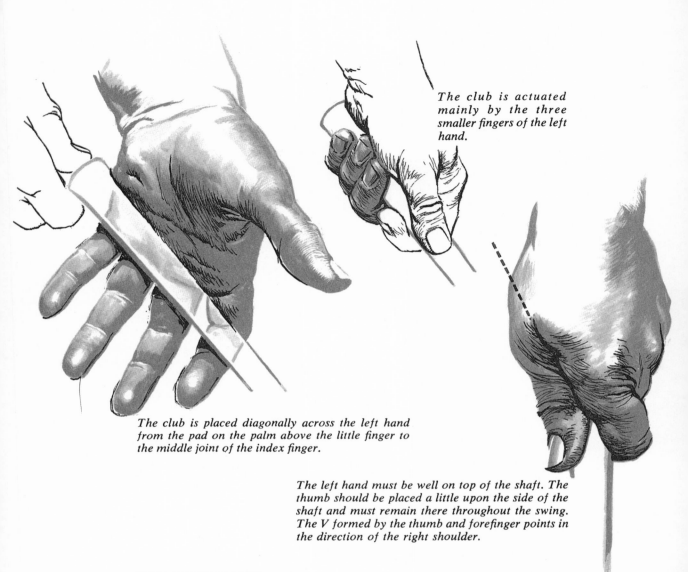

The club is actuated mainly by the three smaller fingers of the left hand.

The club is placed diagonally across the left hand from the pad on the palm above the little finger to the middle joint of the index finger.

The left hand must be well on top of the shaft. The thumb should be placed a little upon the side of the shaft and must remain there throughout the swing. The V formed by the thumb and forefinger points in the direction of the right shoulder.

THE LEFT HAND

In my conception of the golf swing, it is the left arm that starts and controls the direction of the stroke until the time to hit arrives.

For this reason, a firm grip of the left hand is a necessity. The grip of the left hand should be arranged so that the shaft of the club lies diagonally across the palm but is held mainly by the fingers. At the position of address, the club should rest upon the middle joint of the index finger, but the most positive part of the gripping should be done by the two smaller fingers and the middle finger.

The worst mistake possible in gripping the club is to separate the actions of the two hands. They must be placed on the shaft so that they may work together.

Some little latitude is allowable, but it is very small. The left hand must be in a position of power—well on top of the shaft.

Similarly, the right hand must not be placed too far under the shaft because from this position, it may turn over in the act of hitting. Although slight variations are permissible, the right hand should be placed approximately against the side of the shaft.

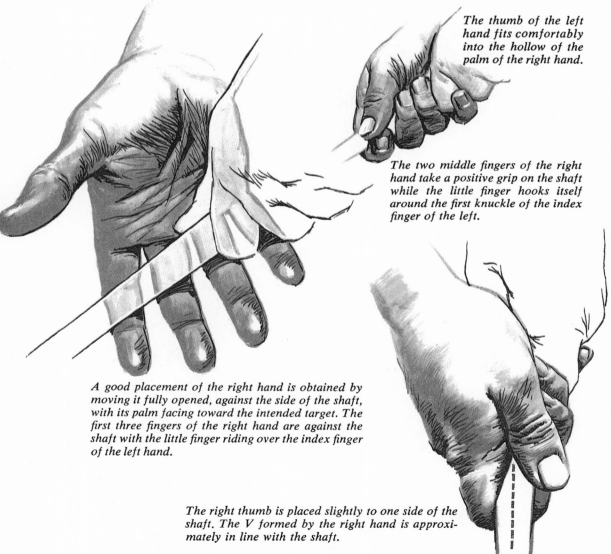

The thumb of the left hand fits comfortably into the hollow of the palm of the right hand.

The two middle fingers of the right hand take a positive grip on the shaft while the little finger hooks itself around the first knuckle of the index finger of the left.

A good placement of the right hand is obtained by moving it fully opened, against the side of the shaft, with its palm facing toward the intended target. The first three fingers of the right hand are against the shaft with the little finger riding over the index finger of the left hand.

The right thumb is placed slightly to one side of the shaft. The V formed by the right hand is approximately in line with the shaft.

11

THE HANDS SHOULD WORK AS A UNIT

Although the grip in which the little finger of the right hand overlaps the index finger of the left is favored by almost all of today's golfers, it is not necessary to distinguish between the overlapping, interlocking, and old-fashioned grips. Any one is good enough if the hands are placed so they can work together.

In all cases, the correct grip must be compact. The two hands must fit closely together upon the shaft. The club is grasped by the fingers, but it is pressed diagonally across the palms of both hands.

The hands should work as a unit, but each hand performs a specific function. Let us simply say that the left hand holds the club on track; the right hand is responsible for timing and touch.

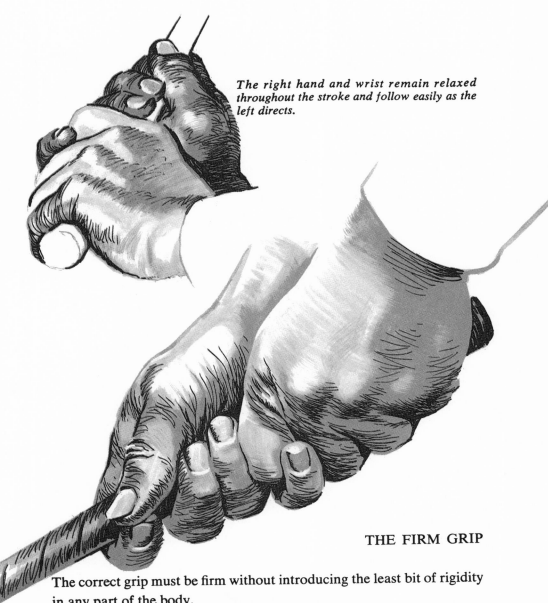

The right hand and wrist remain relaxed throughout the stroke and follow easily as the left directs.

THE FIRM GRIP

The correct grip must be firm without introducing the least bit of rigidity in any part of the body.

The best way to achieve a relaxed grip, which will at the same time maintain adequate control of the club, is to be sure that the left hand has been placed correctly on the shaft. If the greatest pressure is exerted by the last three fingers, the club can be restrained against considerable force, yet the wrist joints may retain complete flexibility. The remainder of the gripping should be done as lightly as possible, exerting pressure upon the shaft only as this becomes necessary in order to move or restrain the club.

2
THE STANCE

Beginning to play a golf shot is addressing the ball and the posture one assumes in doing so is called the address. At address, there must be in the player's mind a very clear picture of the manner and direction in which he intends to hit. As he approaches the ball and places himself before it preparing to strike, he must arrange his posture so that he feels capable of delivering a blow along the desired path.

The essentials of the address position are ease, comfort, and relaxation. Above all else, the first posture must be one from which the movement of the swing may be started smoothly without having to break down successive barriers of tension set up by taut or strained muscles. To go a bit further, the player should feel himself alert, sensitive to impulses, and ready to move in either direction.

Any posture that feels uncomfortable is certain to produce a strain somewhere that will cause the ensuing movement to be jerky. It is well to remember that there are no forces outside the player's own body that have to be resisted or balanced. There is no need for him to set or brace himself, for there is nothing to brace against.

A famous English professional of another era put it quite well when he said, "A golfer must always move freely beneath himself." If this conception should appeal to others as it does to me, it would be a fine thing for the player to have in mind as he addresses the ball.

THE PROCEDURE IN ADDRESSING THE BALL

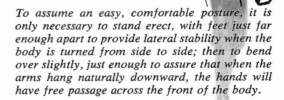

To assume an easy, comfortable posture, it is only necessary to stand erect, with feet just far enough apart to provide lateral stability when the body is turned from side to side; then to bend over slightly, just enough to assure that when the arms hang naturally downward, the hands will have free passage across the front of the body.

Almost all first class players initiate the stance in substantially the same way. The procedure is about like this: The player walks up to the ball from behind, all the while planning the shot he is about to play; as he nears the ball, he will ground his club behind it.

Still aware of his objective, he will place his left foot so as to provide proper alignment and drop the right foot back into a comfortable position.

This preliminary procedure accomplishes several things. First, it fixes the distance from the feet to the ball in the best of all ways by accommodating the distance to the comfortable extent of the arms and club. The second advantage is that the approach to the ball is made in the normal, relaxed manner of ordinary walking; and, approaching the ball from behind, the player is more likely to stop where his body is behind the stroke—an important point we will take up later.

In discussing the basic fundamentals of the proper stance, the player must keep in mind that these details are not to be imitated with complete accuracy. At no time should he try to place each part of the body in a definite position. Any attempt to do so is bound to set up a certain amount of tension. From the first position, it is ease and comfort that must be sought.

At address, the left arm should be straight, or nearly so; the right relaxed.

The correct position from which the complete swing may be most easily accomplished approximates the one we assume when we stand naturally erect. The feet are about twelve inches apart; the ball is on a line with the left heel; the hands of the player are ahead of the ball and the head of the club rests behind the ball.

17

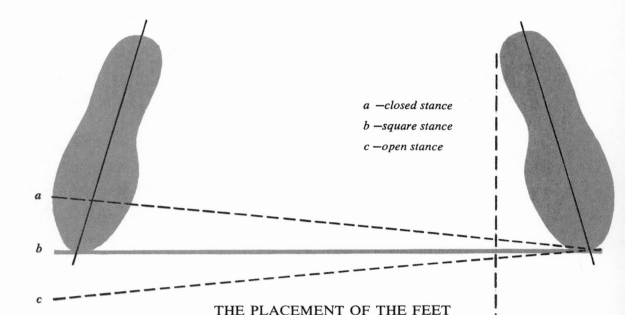

a —closed stance

b —square stance

c —open stance

THE PLACEMENT OF THE FEET

In taking the stance, the feet must be placed so that they do not present any anatomical limitation upon the free swinging movement, either in the backward wind-up or in the forward motion of striking the ball.

This means that the toes of both feet should be turned slightly outward, that is, away from the ball. If this is done, the legs are free to rotate the trunk in either direction. If either foot should be pointed in a direction perpendicular to the line of play, some strain must be put upon it when the swing moves to that side.

In the position of address, the ball should be located so that a line perpendicular to the line of flight passing through the ball would also pass through the heel of the player's left foot, or slightly back of this point.

If the posture of the player at address is natural and comfortable, his weight should be supported about equally by his two feet; this should be so because the swing should rotate around the spine as an axis. In this swinging movement, there is a flow of weight, first backward onto the right heel as the club goes back, and then forward onto the left leg at the finish.

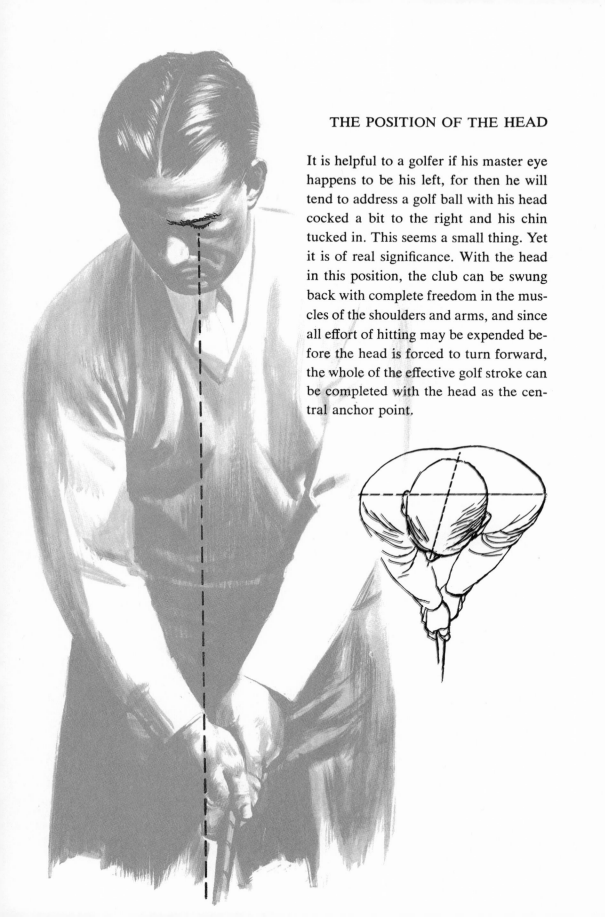

THE POSITION OF THE HEAD

It is helpful to a golfer if his master eye happens to be his left, for then he will tend to address a golf ball with his head cocked a bit to the right and his chin tucked in. This seems a small thing. Yet it is of real significance. With the head in this position, the club can be swung back with complete freedom in the muscles of the shoulders and arms, and since all effort of hitting may be expended before the head is forced to turn forward, the whole of the effective golf stroke can be completed with the head as the central anchor point.

3
THE START *of the* BACKSWING

It is often urged that a person playing golf who worries about how to take the club back, how to start it down, and what to do at this stage and that, ultimately loses sight of the only important thing he has to do—hit the ball. We, who write on the game and those who attempt to teach it, are told often enough that we should give more attention to the contact stage and less to the details of the preparatory movements.

It is a fact, however, that there are certain actions that must take place during the act of hitting if the ball is to be struck with accuracy and power. A haphazard player once in a while may find himself in position to complete these actions, but he cannot hope to compete successfully with the man whose sound swing carries him time after time into this position.

The purpose of the backswing is to establish a perfectly balanced, powerful position at the top of the swing from which the correct actions of the downstroke can flow rhythmically and without the need for interference or correction. In the end, on the basis of consistent reproduction of the successful action, the preparatory movements become just as important as the actual hitting—the entire swing a sequence of correct positions, following naturally and comfortably one after the other.

THE FORWARD PRESS AT THE BEGINNING

A valuable aid in starting the swing smoothly, because it assists in breaking up any tension which may have crept in, is a little forward twist of the hips. Often referred to as the "forward press," its chief function is to assure a smooth start of the swing by setting the hip turn in motion. The movement is in the hips and knees.

The initial movement of the club away from the ball should result from forces originating in the player's left side; the real take-off is from the left foot beginning the backswing. The hands and arms very soon begin to take part, but the proper order of movement is first in the trunk, next in the arms, and lastly in the clubhead. The motion originated by the turn of the hips, followed by the movement of the left arm, causes a break in the approximately straight line from left shoulder to clubhead. This is the drag, and it is the beginning of the leisurely slinging movement characteristic of a smooth swing.

During the early stages of the backswing there is no visible independent action of the hands and wrists. However, in starting the club back, the player should produce a little firming of the left-hand grip, preparing for the pickup to come later.

As the backswing progresses farther, the clubhead catches up and passes through a point where the straight line from left shoulder to clubhead is restored.

With the backswing under way, there is a straightening of the right leg. The left heel is raised only slightly. The hips turn slowly with the hands. The right elbow is close to the side, and the swing goes on with the left hand doing most of the work.

As we reach the halfway point of the backswing, the head remains steady, the shoulders are rotating around a fixed axis, the hips have made a quarter turn, the left knee is moving toward the right, and the left foot is rolling inward pulling the left heel off the ground.

At about this point in the backswing, the hands and arms begin perceptibly to lift the club up to the top of the swing.

Throughout its sweep to the top of the swing, the left arm remains straight, carrying practically all of the burden in moving the clubhead to the crest of its arc. In contrast, the right arm remains as relaxed as possible, leaving the right elbow tucked in close to the side until the upper reaches of the swing draw it away.

If the correct position is taken at address, the weight should be equally apportioned to each foot and evenly distributed over the area of each. From this position, the proper body action is purely a turn or pivot with no shifting or sway whatever.

The raising of the left heel during the backswing must not be considered to be an end in itself; rather, it is to be looked upon as the result of handling the backward wind-up of the body in a correct fashion.

As related to the feet, then, the correct action transfers the weight supported by the left leg to the inside of the foot, and at the top of the swing the left heel has been pulled from the ground and the inside of the ball of the foot is bearing the burden.

To think of starting the backward motion by moving the weight over to the inside of the ball of the left foot is often the easiest way to originate the correct action, for this movement of itself turns the left knee back and forces the turn of the right side.

THE TOP *of the* BACKSWING

One of the characteristics of the true swing, and the one that most often escapes the inexpert player, is the ample sweep of the backward wind-up. The average golfer, partly because he is unfamiliar with the movements that will accommodate a long backswing, and partly because he does not trust himself to go so far, almost always favors a short, hacking stroke. Quickly back and quickly down, employing a sudden acceleration almost amounting to a jerk, there is scarcely any chance of obtaining power or accuracy.

Many players have come to believe that a short backswing, by eliminating some of the body turn, simplifies the stroke to the extent that grave errors will be avoided. I have always held the contrary view. A great many more shots are spoiled by a swing that is too short than by one that is too long.

If we liken the backswing of a golf club to the extension of a coil spring, or the stretching of a rubber band, I think we shall not be very far off our mark. The greater the extension or stretching, the greater the force of the return. In the golf swing, every inch added to the backward wind-up, up to the limit at which the balance of the player can be easily maintained, represents additional stored energy available to increase the power of the downswing.

The player approaches the top of the back-swing by pushing the club back with the left side and arm. When the wind-up is completed, he should feel a tautness up the left side from the left hip to the hand.

At the topmost position, the weight of the clubhead and its momentum will exert a mild tug on the hands and so encourage a full cocking of the wrists. It is at this point that the angle between the straight left arm and the shaft of the club is most acute, and for this reason, the grip of the left hand is under maximum stress.

If the player's grip is correct when he reaches the top of the swing, he will feel the fingers of the left hand give a little; but he will not lose control if he is gripping with the last three fingers of this hand.

The **backswing** *must be accomplished with no swaying or shifting.*

The **head** *remains immovable throughout.*

The **trunk** *rotates around the spine as an axis.*

The **weight,** *though equally distributed between the feet as at address, now rests on the inside of the ball of the left foot, and far back on the outside heel of the right.*

At the top of the swing the shaft of the club, which for the long shots is approximately in a horizontal plane, should at the same time be pointing to a spot slightly to the right of the object at which the player is aiming. This is the result of swinging the club back to the top, rather than lifting it, as so many beginners do.

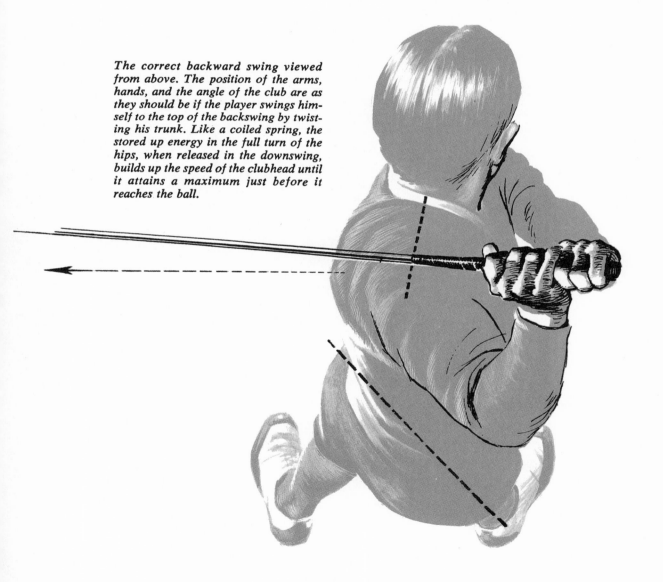

The correct backward swing viewed from above. The position of the arms, hands, and the angle of the club are as they should be if the player swings himself to the top of the backswing by twisting his trunk. Like a coiled spring, the stored up energy in the full turn of the hips, when released in the downswing, builds up the speed of the clubhead until it attains a maximum just before it reaches the ball.

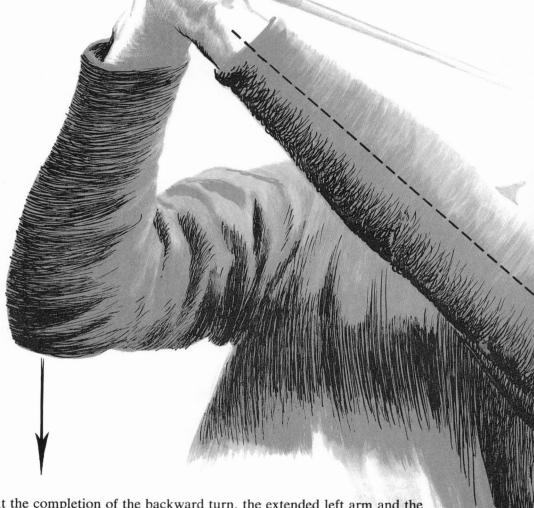

At the completion of the backward turn, the extended left arm and the necessary elevation of the hands, draws the right elbow away from the ribs, where it should have remained until the last possible moment. The elbow is not, however, lifted into the air aimlessly; the right forearm should point obliquely, almost vertically, toward the ground and be drawn away from the side only as much as may be necessary to accommodate a full swing of the club.

At the top of the swing both wrists are under the shaft, the left cocked inward, and the right merely flexed in the direction in which it is easiest for it to move.

It is here that the fingers of the left hand must maintain a positive hold on the club; they must be in control, even though they may open slightly as the swing changes direction.

A high rate of efficiency in golf depends upon the proper use of the left arm. When the left arm is straight, the arc of the backswing is as wide as it can be made, and can be more easily repeated time after time in the same groove. So, let us say that a straight left arm is one of the prime requisites of good form. In many ways, it contributes to clubhead speed, accurate contact, and consistency of performance.

If it is physically impossible for a player to complete a backswing of full length with a straight left arm, he may bend it a little at this point. The important thing, as far as the left arm is concerned, is that it should not collapse in the act of hitting. As long as the player keeps the left arm reasonably extended at the top, it will become completely straight when he initiates the downswing, back toward the ball.

5

THE START *of the* DOWNSWING

The swinging of the club back from the ball is undertaken for the sole purpose of getting the player into a proper position for striking. So the one influence most likely to assure the satisfactory progression of the swing is the clearly visualized contact between club and ball.

I stress this point because I know that the unrelenting effort to play golf in this way can do more for a player than anything he can possibly do. When every move of the swing is dominated by the determination to strike the ball in a definite fashion, the complicated sequence of movements must acquire purpose and unity attainable in no other way.

Up to this point we have been concerned only with the backswing. Now we come to the place where the swing changes direction. Yet, there is no single stage at which all backward or upward movement comes to a halt and a fixed position is attained from which the downswing begins.

As nearly as possible, the backswing and downswing should be blended together so as to compose one movement. The transition from upswing to downswing, therefore, becomes a truly crucial point, for it is here that almost all bad golf shots are incubated. Just let the player's hands move a few inches toward the front, or let him turn his head a few degrees toward the objective and the shot will be spoiled beyond recovery. Even among professionals this is the real danger point of the swing.

THE MOST IMPORTANT MOVEMENT

If we exclude the grip, which in truth is a preliminary, then I should say that the most important movement of the swing is to start the downswing by beginning the unwinding of the hips. There can be no power, and very little accuracy or reliability, in a swing in which the left hip does not lead the downstroke.

No matter how perfect the backswing may have been, if the hands, or the arms, or the shoulders start the downward movement, the club immediately loses the guidance of the body movement, and the benefit of the power the muscles of the waist and back could have contributed. When this happens, the club finds itself in midair, actuated by a pair of hands and arms having no effective connection with anything solid. I think we may well call the unwinding of the hips the most important movement of the swing.

In any full swing, correctly performed, the trunk will begin to unwind while the hands and club are still going back. This order of movement has the effect of accomplishing two very important results. First, of course, it causes the hip-turn to lead the downstroke and so make the power generated by the reverse turn of the body usable in the form of club head momentum. But equally important is the effect of completing the cocking of the wrists. This is accomplished as the wrists give to the pull of the hips in one direction and of the club head moving in the other. As the downstroke begins, one should have the feel of leaving the clubhead at the top.

Since the downstroke is led by the unwinding of the trunk, the left side again becomes the focal point. If complete use is to be made of the power latent in the player's leg and back muscles, there must be a sense of pulling or stretching up the left side and arm to the grip end of the club.

THE WEIGHT SHIFT

Although there is no apparent shifting of weight from left foot to right during the backstroke, there is a decided transference of weight to the left side when the swing changes direction from up to down.

The shifting of a preponderance of weight to the left foot in the downswing should be simultaneous with the unwinding of the trunk, and like the hip-turn, is executed quickly, leading the arms and club all the way through.

But it must be just that—a shift, not a sway. The difference should be clearly understood. It is this: The weight shift which is proper is a shift of the hips—a lateral movement of the middle part of the body that does not alter the location of the head and shoulders with respect to the ball; the sway, which is improper, is a forward movement of the entire body, that sends the head and shoulders forward too, and tends to upset the player's balance.

The unwinding of the hips in the correct swing is very rapid indeed. They begin to unwind— that is to turn back toward the ball—even before the club has reached the end of its backward travel. As a result, the left leg begins to straighten and the left heel to return to the ground very early in the downswing while the hands are at shoulder level or above.

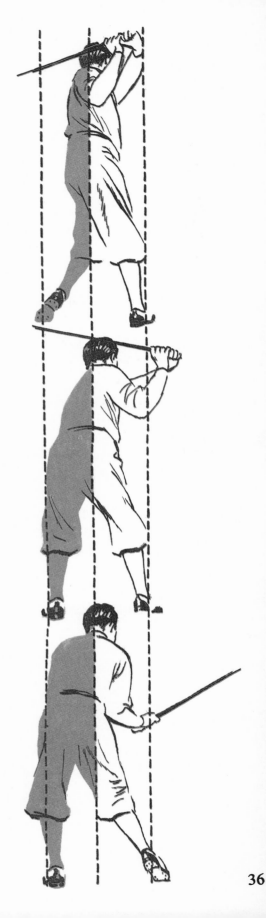

THE RETURN OF THE RIGHT ELBOW

The point at which the swing changes direction from up to down is one of those spots where the motion slows down enough so that a bit of conscious control may be applied. A very important maneuver at this point is to make certain of returning the elbow of the right arm back to the side of the body as the downswing commences, at the same time relaxing the right wrist and thereby increasing its inward set. This has the effect of dropping the club a bit toward the player's rear and thus increasing the chances of hitting straight through the ball on the line of flight.

6
THE DOWNSWING

Hitting with the right hand from the top of the swing ruins as many shots as any other single fault. By forcing the downswing out beyond its proper groove, and by using up the cock of the wrists too quickly, it can lead to almost anything from a smothered hook to a full-fledged shank. When the right hand takes charge at the top, there is no possibility of approaching the ball from inside the line of play—and nearly every golfer is inclined to do this, especially when he is trying to hit hard.

The remedy or preventive involves two main intentions: first, to relax the right arm as completely as possible during the backswing, and second, to begin the downswing at a moderate pace, no matter how hard you intend to hit.

If one merely thinks of dropping the right elbow back to the side, while the wrists retain their cocking, the momentum will come from the unwinding of the hips and speed can be built up and used in an effective way.

Unwinding the hips while the club is still moving in the opposite direction exerts a pull against the inertia of the clubhead, stretches the left arm taut, and takes up the slack between the left hip and the left hand. Under these conditions, any further movement of the hips is immediately, and without loss, communicated to the clubhead.

By rapidly returning the hips to the address-position and beyond, the upper part of the body, actuated by the hip-turn, is virtually pulled around in one piece almost to the hitting position. This movement reduces to a minimum any possibility of hitting from the top, and because this point in the downswing is reached without any activity of the hands, the cocking of the wrists has been preserved substantially intact.

The right arm is relaxed as it was at the top, and the right elbow is still tucked against the ribs of the player's side. The right hand is in readiness to unleash its power.

Up to this point, club head acceleration has been contributed to only by the unwinding of the hips and the movement of the left arm by which it has caught up a little bit on the hip-turn.

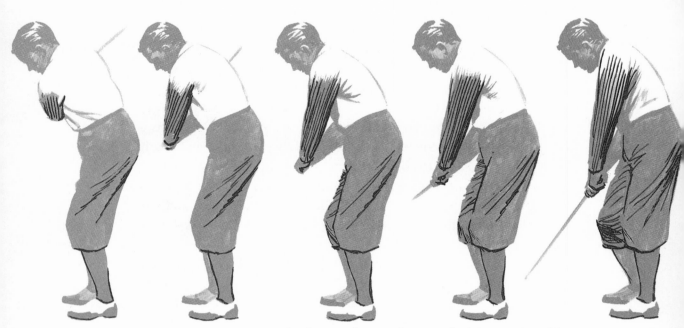

As soon as the hip-turn of the downstroke is under way, the left arm should be straight, and remain so until after the ball has been struck. The left arm should work closely across the chest and front, but there must never be any suggestion of the player's "hugging himself" with it.

40

When the swing is about halfway down, the player passes through a semisquatting posture when the hands are waist high on the downstroke. From this point on, there is a straightening of the left leg that culminates in a powerful thrust immediately prior to contact. Inevitably, this movement tends to straighten the right leg as well.

An ample cocking of the wrists, and the retention of the greater part of this angle for use in the hitting area is not only important for good timing and increasing the speed of the club head, it is absolutely necessary in order to enable the player to strike downward and so produce backspin.

7
IMPACT

When we speak of a sound swing or of good form, we mean nothing more than that the possessor has simplified his swing to the point where errors are less likely to creep in, and he is able consistently to bring his club against the ball in the correct hitting position. We talk, think, and write so much about the details of the stroke that we sometimes lose sight of the one thing that is all important—hitting the ball.

The only reason for discussing method and form at all is to find a way to make it easier for the player to achieve the correct relation to the ball at impact. In a crude way, he might do it only occasionally; in a finished, sound, controlled way, he will be able to do it consistently and with assurance.

The beginner ought to keep always before him the determination to put the club against the ball in the correct position. It is not easy when form is lacking, but it is the surest way to cause form to be more easily acquired.

The right hand remains relaxed and cocked until the angle between the left arm and the shaft of the club is about ninety degrees. It is from this position to the point of contact with the ball that the straightening of the wrists and the final violent completion of the unwinding of the trunk produce the maximum striking effort.

As nearly as I can describe the sensation of striking a golf ball, it is a combination of a pull through with the left side, combined with a slapping action with the right hand and forearm, the left being responsible for keeping the swing on the track or groove, and the right being responsible for bringing the movement to a well-timed climax as the ball is struck.

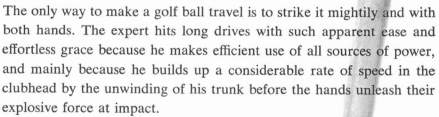

The only way to make a golf ball travel is to strike it mightily and with both hands. The expert hits long drives with such apparent ease and effortless grace because he makes efficient use of all sources of power, and mainly because he builds up a considerable rate of speed in the clubhead by the unwinding of his trunk before the hands unleash their explosive force at impact.

The golfer must strike strongly with his right hand, but he must first put his hands, both of them, in position to strike in the desired direction. This is done as the swing changes direction at the top. Initiating the downswing with the unwinding of the trunk provides space and time for the hands to drop down along the proper plane whence they may strike toward the objective. Once this move is made, there is no need to hold anything back.

A tremendous amount of power can be derived from a proper use of the hips, legs, and the muscles of the back. In the correct swing, the left hip leads the movement back to the ball, generating speed and power as the unwinding progresses. At the instant of impact, the hips have turned through their position at address; the left arm is swinging through straight along the line of play; the right hand has neither passed nor climbed over the left.

The unwinding of the hips culminates in a sort of wrench just before the club meets the ball, both legs combining to produce a sudden and powerful thrust up the left side of the body.

I like to think of a golf club as a weight attached to my hands by an imponderable medium, to which a string is a close approximation, and I like to feel that I am throwing it at the ball with much the same motion I would use in cracking a whip. By the simile, I mean to convey the idea of a supple and lightning quick action of the hands in striking—a sort of flailing action.

8
THE FOLLOW THROUGH

The whole force of a sound swing is not dissipated at the ball. It is desirable that the blow should be directed through the ball, not merely at it. The feeling is that the clubhead, having built up its full speed, is merely floating through the last little space immediately prior to contact. The moment one feels an awareness of having to hit—the need of an extra effort—the hands tighten upon the club, resistance is set up, and the motion is slowed down rather than accelerated.

The easy, and usually graceful, pose in which the correct golf swing comes to an end is the result of this relaxed swinging. Muscles that have not been tightened in the effort of hitting do not tighten up to stop the club. When the swing has passed through the ball, the work has been done, the impulse is withdrawn, and the momentum of the club simply draws a compliant body around to the finish of the swing.

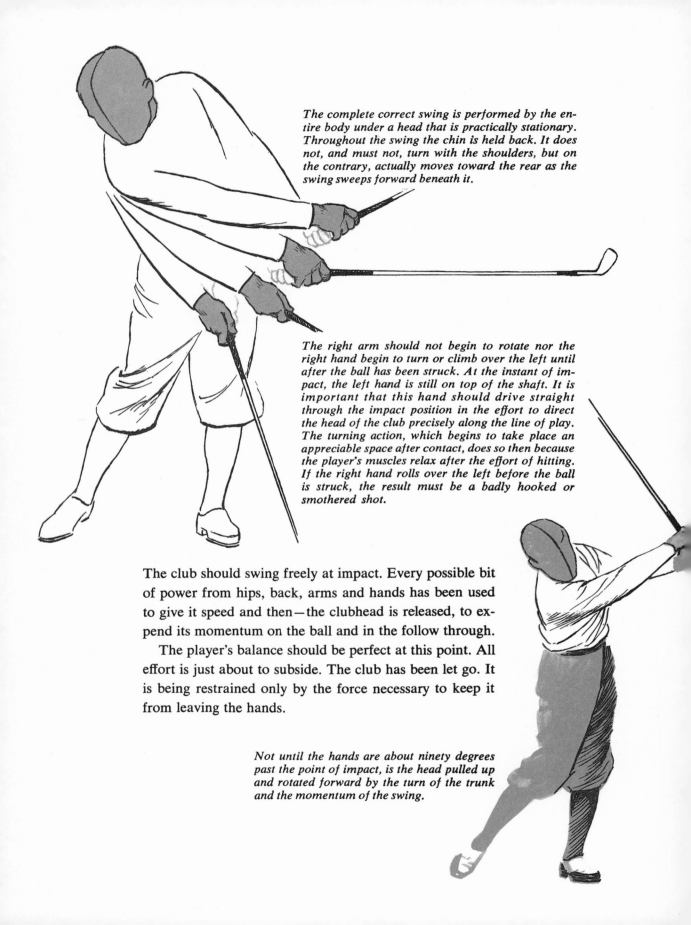

The complete correct swing is performed by the entire body under a head that is practically stationary. Throughout the swing the chin is held back. It does not, and must not, turn with the shoulders, but on the contrary, actually moves toward the rear as the swing sweeps forward beneath it.

The right arm should not begin to rotate nor the right hand begin to turn or climb over the left until after the ball has been struck. At the instant of impact, the left hand is still on top of the shaft. It is important that this hand should drive straight through the impact position in the effort to direct the head of the club precisely along the line of play. The turning action, which begins to take place an appreciable space after contact, does so then because the player's muscles relax after the effort of hitting. If the right hand rolls over the left before the ball is struck, the result must be a badly hooked or smothered shot.

The club should swing freely at impact. Every possible bit of power from hips, back, arms and hands has been used to give it speed and then—the clubhead is released, to expend its momentum on the ball and in the follow through.

The player's balance should be perfect at this point. All effort is just about to subside. The club has been let go. It is being restrained only by the force necessary to keep it from leaving the hands.

Not until the hands are about ninety degrees past the point of impact, is the head pulled up and rotated forward by the turn of the trunk and the momentum of the swing.

We all hope that the posture at the finish will be an expression of ease, grace and balance. It can only be so if we have followed a proper order of movement throughout the entire swing.

The appearance of the player at the end of his effort will betray his inconsistencies or confirm his perfection.

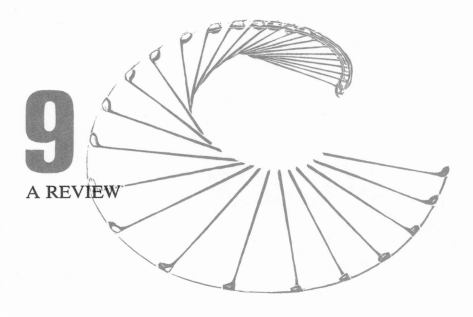

9

A REVIEW

Since the immediate purpose of this book is to provide a broad, general appreciation of the golf swing as a whole, I think it might be helpful to review the main points in the basic elements of the swing. It is important, especially for the beginner, to have a clear picture of these points indelibly stamped in his mind. Of equal importance, a condensed version of the proper sequence enables the reader to grasp the conception of a swing in which each essential movement flows smoothly into each succeeding essential.

In presenting the fundamentals, the matters of grip, stance, backswing, and downswing are, of necessity, treated separately. But when actually swinging a club, there should be no conscious effort to pass by rote through a series of prescribed positions. The whole thing happens too fast to be subject to this degree of control.

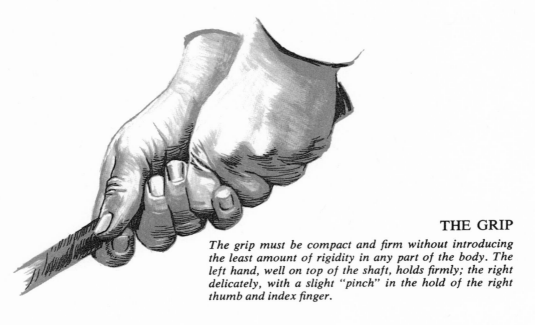

THE GRIP

The grip must be compact and firm without introducing the least amount of rigidity in any part of the body. The left hand, well on top of the shaft, holds firmly; the right delicately, with a slight "pinch" in the hold of the right thumb and index finger.

THE STANCE

The player should address the ball in a perfectly natural position. Feet not too far apart, body only slightly bent over, arms hanging naturally down, weight equally distributed between the feet and balance so perfect that no sense of strain is felt in any muscle.

THE BACKSWING

Hands and club are started back by the rotation of the trunk and the movement of the arms.

At about point (a) the player should firm the left hand, preparing for the pickup to come later.

At about point (b) the hands and arms begin perceptibly to lift the club up to the top of the swing.

At point (c), as the hands approach the topmost position, the weight of the club-head and its momentum will exert a mild tug on the hands and so encourage a full cocking of the wrists; but the player will not lose control if he is gripping with the three smaller fingers of the left hand.

The weight (d) at the top of the swing, rests on the inside of the ball of the left foot, and far back on the outside of the heel of the right.

The head remains immovable throughout, the trunk rotates around the spine as an axis.

The plane of the backswing in a properly executed golf stroke. Note that the left arm, which should be straight at address, remains straight, or nearly so, throughout the swing. When the left arm is straight, the arc of the backswing is as wide as it can be made, and can more easily be repeated time after time in the same groove.

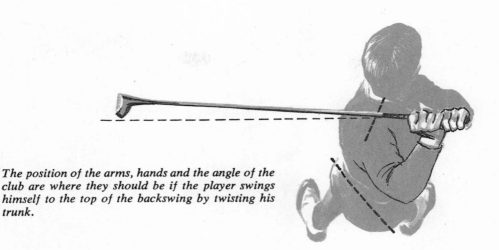

The position of the arms, hands and the angle of the club are where they should be if the player swings himself to the top of the backswing by twisting his trunk.

At the completion of the full backward turn, the left heel has been pulled from the ground, the straight left arm has drawn the right elbow away from the ribs where it should have remained until the last possible moment, both wrists are under the shaft, and the right elbow points downward.

THE DOWNSWING IS INITIATED BY THE
UNWINDING OF THE HIPS. *There can be no
power, and very little accuracy or reliability, in a
swing in which the left hip does not lead the downstroke. The all-important feel which the player
should experience is one of leaving the clubhead at
the top of the swing.*

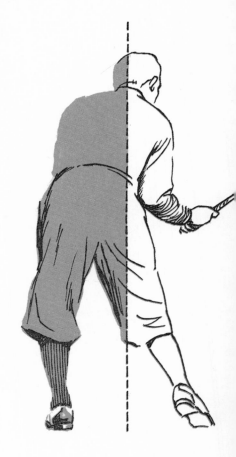

*Almost simultaneous with the hip-turn, which is ex-
ecuted quickly, is the return of the right elbow to the
side of the body, the transference of a preponderance of weight to the left side, the grounding of the
left heel and the straightening of the left leg.*

The downswing is on the same plane as the backswing. But the arc formed by the clubhead moves to the left as a result of the weight shift and the retention of the wrist cock during the early stages of the downstroke. The wrists do not begin to straighten until the hands enter the hitting zone at about point (a).

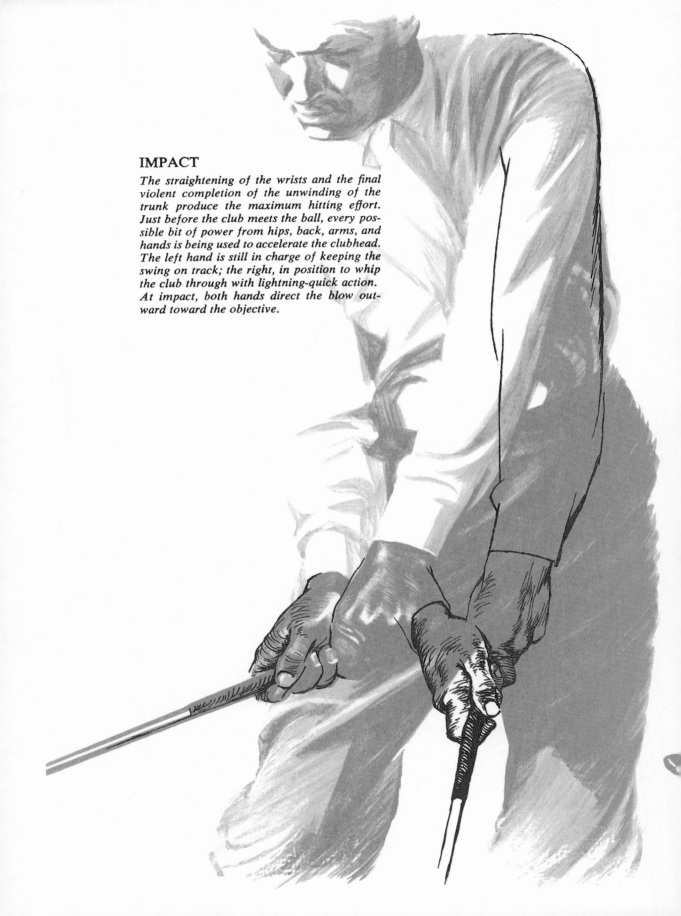

IMPACT

*The straightening of the wrists and the final
violent completion of the unwinding of the
trunk produce the maximum hitting effort.
Just before the club meets the ball, every possible bit of power from hips, back, arms, and
hands is being used to accelerate the clubhead.
The left hand is still in charge of keeping the
swing on track; the right, in position to whip
the club through with lightning-quick action.
At impact, both hands direct the blow outward toward the objective.*

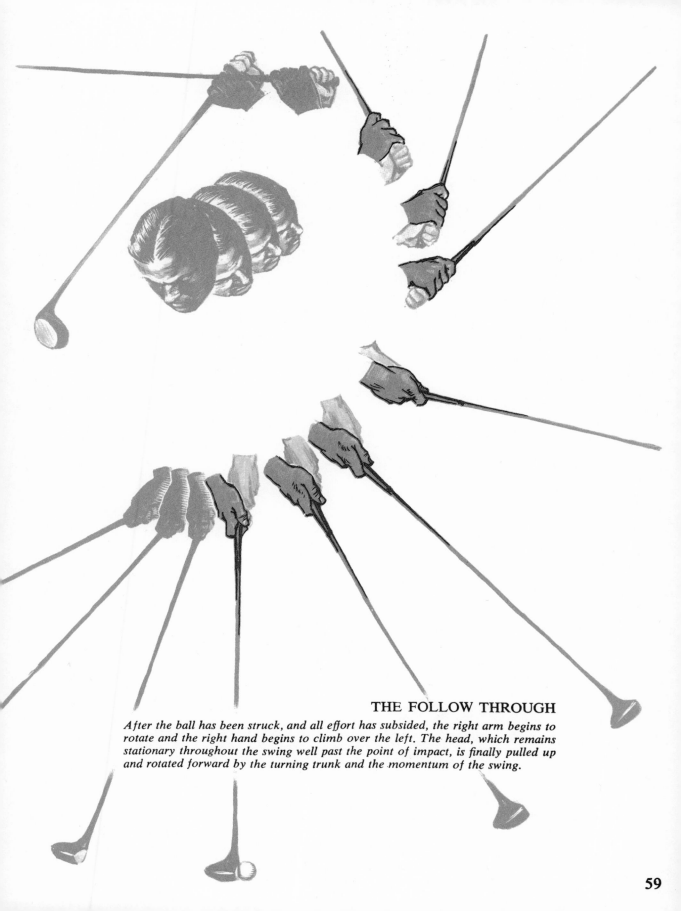

THE FOLLOW THROUGH

After the ball has been struck, and all effort has subsided, the right arm begins to rotate and the right hand begins to climb over the left. The head, which remains stationary throughout the swing well past the point of impact, is finally pulled up and rotated forward by the turning trunk and the momentum of the swing.

59

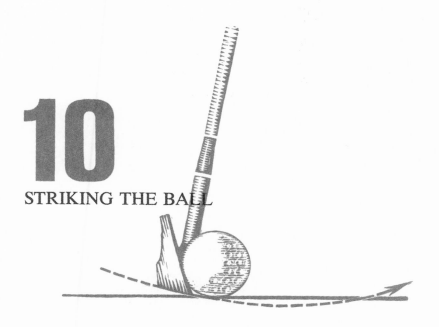

10

STRIKING THE BALL

Golf is played by striking the ball with the head of the club. The objective of the player is not to swing the club in a specified manner, nor to execute a series of complicated movements in a prescribed sequence, nor to look pretty while he is doing it, but primarily and essentially to strike the ball with the head of the club so that the ball will perform according to his wishes.

No one can play golf until he knows the many ways in which a golf ball can be expected to respond when it is struck in different ways. If you think that all this should be obvious, please believe me when I assure you that I have seen many good players attempt shots they should have known were impossible.

If you are a beginner, this information will start you off on the road to a correct understanding of the nature of golf. If you are an average golfer, it will give you the means of deciding upon the shot to play on the basis of reasoned judgment, rather than guesswork. If you are a better than average golfer, it will broaden your perception of the possibilities in the game so that you may become a player of imagination and resourcefulness. If you are weary of being told to concentrate without having knowledge of what you should concentrate on, this is it.

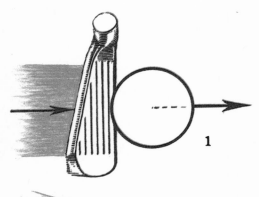

Diagram 1 is intended to represent a ball being struck by a clubhead moving precisely along the intended line of flight with its face square to the objective. In the absence of wind, the only possible result is a straight shot directly on target. This is ideal for most golfing situations.

1

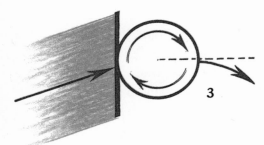

Diagram 2 depicts the result when the player actually succeeds in hitting across the line of flight from the inside to out. As a practical matter, it is not possible to slide the face of the club across the ball in this direction, but the mere fact that the back of the ball has been compressed on the side nearest the player will cause it to spin in a counterclockwise direction and therefore to HOOK.

2

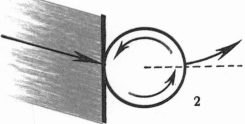

Diagram 3 shows a ball being struck by a clubhead moving from outside the line of flight across to the inside, while its face is aligned at an angle of more than ninety degrees to the direction of its travel. This sort of contact will produce a SLICE, which is a curve to the right for the right-handed player. If the error is small, a satisfactory result may be had, because the curved flight so produced may serve only to correct for the original impetus in the other direction.

3

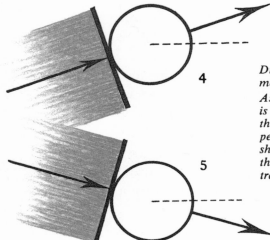

4

Diagrams 4 and 5 are included mainly to illustrate the meaning of two common terms—PULL and PUSH.

As will appear inevitable from diagram 4, the PULL is a shot which does not curve, but flies to the left of the objective because the face of the club is aligned perpendicular to the direction of the blow. The PUSHED shot flies straight to the right for the same reason. With the face of the club aligned squarely to the line of its travel, no side-spin is imparted to the ball.

5

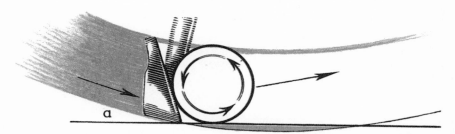

In playing to the green, it becomes important to adjust the range of the shot within close limits. For this purpose, three variables are available to us—the choice of the club to be used, the decision whether to swing the club at full strength or less, and the employment of backspin.

BACKSPIN is produced by striking the ball a descending blow (a). The angle of loft of the face of the club makes possible a point of contact below the center line of the ball so that the force of the blow is exerted partly in propelling the ball forward, and partly in causing it to spin. Since the spin is produced by the gripping effect between club and ball, the contact must be clean. The divot is taken after the ball has been struck.

If the contact between club and ball be anywhere near flush, it is very nearly impossible that some backspin should not result. Diagram (b) shows the only way a ball can be struck without backspin. In the teed-up shot, the contact is such that its force is directed on a radius to the center of the ball so that no spinning effect results.

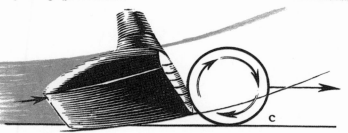

The average golfer, when playing a wood club from the fairway, never thinks of it as a backspin shot. He tries to get under the ball and lift it into the air. Result: he either catches the club in the ground, or, if he misses the ground (c), he commits a half or full top of the ball.

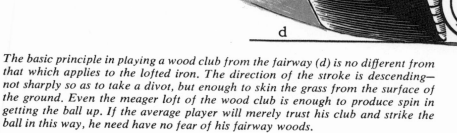

The basic principle in playing a wood club from the fairway (d) is no different from that which applies to the lofted iron. The direction of the stroke is descending—not sharply so as to take a divot, but enough to skin the grass from the surface of the ground. Even the meager loft of the wood club is enough to produce spin in getting the ball up. If the average player will merely trust his club and strike the ball in this way, he need have no fear of his fairway woods.

Afterword
by
Charles R. Yates

After rereading this magnificent instructional book by Bob Jones, I think back to a lecture at the Atlanta Historical Society held just prior to the 1990 Masters. The subject of the evening was "Bob Jones and the Early Days of the Masters". On the podium were Byron Nelson and Alistair Cooke. The program started with the showing of a fifteen minute selection of sequences from Bob's instructional movies made back in 1931.

Byron was then asked to compare Bob's technique with the way professional golfers now play so effectively. Byron's response was that Bob was far ahead of his time. He was the first person to develop the modern technique of using the large muscles of one's body rather than pronating in the classic old Scottish style. Byron did state that the one main difference between Bob's swing and that of players almost sixty years later was that Bob was looser at the top than the modern players, who are more controlled. Yet, Byron said, Bob had developed an innate ability to control the club at the top of his swing. This was very noticeable in the film when Bob was playing brassie shots from a fairway to a green 243 yards away. He was hitting the ball uniformly to the green and, most of the time, within a few yards of the pin.

Many golfers have the idea that the modern golf swing has been discovered only in the last few years. Then you study this instructional book and realize that some of the great truths, in golf as in life, go back a long time. Witness what we have learned from the Bible or from the works of Shakespeare, after first believing it is we who have unearthed certain kernels of wisdom. My hope in this Afterword is to give you a sense, a feeling, an idea of what a great man Bob Jones was and how much I treasured his friendship over a period of many years.

As a child, I grew up around the East Lake Country Club where Bob played regularly. He was eleven years older than I was, and I first recall slipping across the fence at the fourth tee and following behind him when he was just seventeen. He was mature far beyond his years and was extraordinarily kind to a youngster like myself. He was the first one to take me into the locker room and buy me that great elixir of Atlanta—Coca-Cola. After finishing a round, Bob would often give us youngsters some balls, and, on occasion, he would go over and play with us on the little chip-and-putt course that was just behind the 18th green. He exemplified the truth of that well-known saying: "A man never stands so tall as when he stoops to help a boy". I also recall that, in Bob's teenage years and later, he had no long sessions on the practice tee but, for the main part, honed his game by frequent playing. The only way I can explain his matchless skill is that he had a God-given natural ability that did not require knocking out buckets of balls on the range.

In the 1925 U. S. Open, Bob lost in a playoff against Willie Macfarlane. The middle of the following week, he was back home playing at East Lake. Then eleven years old, I went up to him and said, "I'm sorry you lost." I will never forget his reply: "Son, always remember you never know who your friends are until you lose."

The history of Bob and his family is fascinating. He was actually named for his grandfather, Robert Tyre Jones, of Canton, Georgia. In that tiny north Georgia community, Mr. Jones was lord of all he surveyed. He was president of the bank and owned a cotton mill as well as the Jones Mercantile Company, which took care of customers in a wide shopping area. I called Bob's mother Miss Clara. For most of her life, she was quite fragile and sickly. On the other hand, Bob's dad, universally known as "The Colonel", was the greatest extrovert in the world. He loved life, and his language was colorful, to say the least. There was a marvelous relationship between father and son. I had the privilege of often playing with Bob and The Colonel commencing in the early 1930s and running until the time Bob retired from golf in 1948, after he had undergone two unsuccessful operations for a rare disease that caused a deterioration of his spine.

I still chuckle over some of the happenings involving The Colonel. One day he topped a tee shot that went about a hundred and twenty-five yards. He backed away and took a practice swing. Then he turned to his son and said: "What's wrong with that swing?". Bob replied, "Nothing, Dad. Why don't you try it some time". Then, just before World War II, a left-handed Methodist preacher named Pierce Harris, who was an excellent golfer, came to Atlanta. Pierce and I used to play Bob and The Colonel. This particular day, Bob shot a 64 and came within one stroke of matching his own course record. The Colonel, on the other hand, was having a terrible time. On the sixteenth hole, he topped his ball into a sand trap, took two to get out, was then bunkered in front of the green, and finally three-putted for eight. Choice words were said after each swing. In the meantime, Bob knocked in a birdie three to close out the match. Walking over to the seventeenth tee, the preacher said to me in a voice that was loud enough to go back to The Colonel and his son: "Charlie, we should have known that we could not compete today against such a combination of proficiency and profanity".

However, the all-time best story about The Colonel took place one afternoon in the early days of the Masters when Cliff Roberts, finding himself short of a Rules Committeeman, asked The Colonel to go out to the most sensitive spot on the course, the twelfth hole. All golfers who watch the Masters are familiar with this dastardly par-3 where one shoots over Rae's Creek to a very narrow green. That day we had heavy rains and the em-

bedded ball rule was in effect, meaning that if a ball was buried anywhere outside a hazard, one was entitled to a lift.

The Colonel was standing behind the eleventh green when he suddenly heard the call for a Rules Committeeman to come to the twelfth green. The Colonel went there and saw a player standing at the bank wanting to know if he was outside the hazard and, therefore, entitled to a lift. He asked The Colonel if the imbedded ball rule was in effect, and The Colonel had not the slightest idea about this rule. Therefore, Colonel Jones countered: "Let me ask you a question, son. How do you stand with par?" The player replied: "Well, sir, today I am seven over and, for the tournament, twenty-three over". The Colonel responded: "Hell, son, I don't give a damn what you do with it—put the son-of-a-bitch on the green for all I care".

Over the years, I have often thought about the great success Bob had on the links and what a rough time he and his family went through in so many different ways. His lovely wife, Mary, was taken by cancer as was their youngest daughter, Mary Ellen. Bob III passed away many years ago due to a heart attack. I am happy to report that his oldest daughter, Clara, is still alive and well and never looked better than when she was down to the recent lecture at the Historical Society.

I must relate to you that Bob was a brilliant person with a tremendous gift for expressing himself in concise language. He had a degree in mechanical engineering from Georgia Tech, another degree for his post-graduate work in the liberal arts at Harvard, and he attended the Law School at Emory University in Atlanta. In less than two years he had accumulated so much legal knowledge that he passed the State Bar Exam and never went back to finish the usual third year.

Although Bob was often asked to play golf exhibitions for charity, what he treasured most was being with his long-time friends, both on and off the course. I have a vivid memory of riding to Augusta with him just prior to World War II. He was talking about these continuous demands for appearing at exhibitions, playing with strangers, and so forth. He said, "Charlie, I really do like people but I like them best in small doses".

In 1948, because of his illness, Bob did have to give up playing golf. When a reporter asked him one time if this didn't trouble him, he said: "It's not all bad. Just think, I'll never again have to worry about a three foot putt." From that year on, Bob endured the worst of times after previously having had just about the best. He handled his illness with great dignity and never wanted anyone to wait on him or worry unduly about him. His office, in the C & S Bank Building, was a small one and one might have imagined that on the walls there would have been many photographs of famous people with whom he had played, and on the shelves various trophies he had won. Actually, there was no golf memorabilia except two things: one was a line drawing of the Old Course at St. Andrews, and the other was a framed picture which showed an attic scene with an old golf bag leaning up against a chair, some wood-shafted clubs sticking out the top, and a battered golf cap hanging over the driver. Alongside was that magnificent poem by Grantland Rice:

"For when the one great scorer comes to write against your name,
    He writes not that you won or lost but how you played the game."

Charles R. Yates